8 25

MEGALITHS
IN
HISTORY

THIS IS THE FOURTH OF THE
WALTER NEURATH MEMORIAL LECTURES
WHICH WILL BE GIVEN ANNUALLY EACH SPRING ON
SUBJECTS REFLECTING THE INTERESTS OF
THE FOUNDER
OF THAMES AND HUDSON

THE DIRECTORS WISH TO EXPRESS
PARTICULAR GRATITUDE TO THE GOVERNORS AND
MASTER OF BIRKBECK COLLEGE,
UNIVERSITY OF LONDON,
FOR THEIR GRACIOUS SPONSORSHIP OF
THESE LECTURES

MEGALITHS
IN
HISTORY

GLYN DANIEL

THAMES AND HUDSON
LONDON

Fifteen years ago I was lunching with Walter Neurath, the initiator of so many excellent books on art and archaeology, whose name and achievement we annually remember in these lectures. It was the time when we were starting the 'Ancient Peoples and Places' series, which he had asked me to edit, and which his wife Eva was designing. I was on my way to lecture in Aarhus and Copenhagen on the history of ideas about megalithic monuments. Walter asked, 'But what happened to megaliths after prehistory? Why don't you lecture about megaliths in history?' I said I would one day, and, keeping my promise, I delivered this lecture at Birkbeck College on 9 March this year. He, alas, did not live to hear it, or to publish it, but his encouragement, his personal kindnesses and sympathetic understanding I shall never forget; they are the inspiration behind this Fourth Walter Neurath Memorial Lecture.

1 *Artist's impression of Stonehenge in 1750*

THE MEGALITHIC MONUMENTS of the west Mediterranean, western Europe and north Europe have interested scholars and the general public from the beginnings of antiquarian speculation in the sixteenth century, although it was not until the middle of the nineteenth century that these great rude and rough stone structures were grouped together under the name of 'megaliths'. There are, broadly speaking, five types of prehistoric monument customarily grouped together as megaliths: first, the menhir or single standing stone; second, groups of standing stones set in rows of which the Carnac alignments in southern Brittany are the most renowned; third, the circular setting of large stones of which the most famous examples in Europe are Stonehenge and Avebury in Wiltshire; fourth, the buildings or chamber tombs walled and roofed with megaliths (or sometimes with a corbel vault); and fifth, the apsidal temples of Malta.

The first few illustrations will remind the reader of these main types. The stone circles cannot be considered apart from the wooden circles now surviving only as post-holes in the ground; the wooden and stone circles with surrounding banks and ditches have been conveniently referred to as 'henge monuments' since Sir Thomas Kendrick suggested that word in the twenties following the discovery by air photography of the site known as 'Woodhenge' a few miles from Stonehenge. Prehistoric chamber tombs survive in two forms: sometimes the chambers are free-standing, that is to say, unencumbered by a covering of earth and stones; at other times they survive partly or completely covered in a mound of earth or stones.

It is not my concern here to discuss megaliths in their prehistoric contexts but only what happened to them subsequently in the beliefs and practices of protohistoric and historic people; we must, however,

7

2 *Alignments at Carnac, Morbihan, Brittany*

be clear as to the date of megalith building in Europe. A quarter of a century ago, most textbooks would attribute megaliths to 'the Late Neolithic and Early Bronze Age' and translate these vague phrases into absolute dates of between say 2200 and 1600 BC. These dates were guesses. The advent of Carbon 14 dating after the last war and its calibration with the dendrochronology provided by the bristlecone pine of California has enabled us to see that megalithic architecture was practised in western Europe for over two thousand years, beginning at 4000 BC or earlier.[1] A tradition of prehistoric building, and the religious beliefs that inspired it, which lasted for over twenty centuries might well be thought to have survived, in some shape or form, into history.

8

3 *Menhirs near Carnac,*
Morbihan, Brittany

4 *Apsidal temples at Hagar Qim,*
Malta

5 The 'allée couverte'
or long megalithic
grave at Essé near
Rennes, Brittany

6 A typical dolmen in
Charente, France

7 Cemetery of chambered
barrows at Lough Crew,
Ireland

10

II

8 *The corbelled roof of the main chamber in the passage grave at New Grange, Ireland*

It is this survival and the re-use of megaliths that is my concern here. A few people, but not many, have had the courage and interest to write about these matters. A hundred years ago there was published the first general book in English about megaliths: this was *Rude Stone Monuments in all Countries: their Age and Uses* by James Fergusson, and it was a by-product of his interest in the general history of architecture. Some forty years later T. E. Peet produced the second general survey in the English language, *Rough Stone Monuments and their Builders*. Fergusson had strange views about the dating of megaliths, and thought those in France were Gallo-Roman. Peet was wiser and argued for a prehistoric date. Both writers were intrigued by the edicts of the early Church Councils, and by the strange monument on the island of Sainte-Marguerite at Confolens on the River Vienne, and it is indeed a strange monument, the gibbous capstone of what the French call, in folk parlance, a 'dolmen' supported on pillars of the twelfth century A D. Adrien de Mortillet wrote an article 'Les Monuments Mégalithiques Christianisés' in 1897,[2] and drew our attention to the great Christianized menhir of Pleumeur-Bodou and the Chapelle des Septs-Saints at Plouaret in the Côtes-du-Nord department of Brittany. Hadrian Allcroft's *The Circle and the Cross* (vol. I, 1927; vol. II, 1930) was full of fascinating suggestions about the survival of prehistoric structures into Christian history. I am not forgetting that in 1902 Wood-Martin called his book on Irish megaliths *Traces of the Elder Faiths,* and then ten years later Walter Johnson referred to many of these matters in his book *Byways in British Archaeology.*

One or two archaeologists have argued that megaliths did not cease being built in the second millennium B C and were built in the Early Iron Age and in Roman times. Dr Joseph Raftery argued that Carn H at Lough Crew in Ireland was built by La Tène Celts, and Miss V. C. C. Collum believed that two monuments which she excavated, one, Tressé, in Brittany, and the other, the Déhus, in Guernsey, were Gallo-Roman in date. The archaeological evidence, on which these late datings is based, is unconvincing.[3] What is, however, certain is that there is plenty of Roman material in the chambered tombs of north-western Europe. What does this mean? That there were Gallo-Roman antiquarian groups interested in megaliths? That Gallo-Romans had picnic parties in ancient tombs? Or does it mean a survival of the elder faiths or even a cult of ancient religious places? Sometimes it is quite clear that old megalithic tombs were used to live in. The village of Plou-fragan is near Saint-Brieuc on the Roman road from Corseul to Carhaix. Here in 1854 was excavated an *allée couverte*, or long megalithic tomb, presumably dating from the second millennium BC. It was divided into three compartments and the middle one had been transformed into a makeshift dwelling for a wealthy Gallo-Roman who had got in by removing one of the partly broken roof-slabs. A room had been constructed with a brick floor; under the Gallo-Roman floor were remains of the La Tène Iron Age.[4]

Two graves found by Colonel Hawley at Stonehenge were probably Romano-British. Professor Atkinson thinks the ruin of Stonehenge is due in part to deliberate destruction during the Roman occupation of Britain and adduces some evidence of the breaking up of stones in the Roman period.[5]

There is good evidence in Ireland of the taking over of passage-grave hill-tops by Iron Age people, for example at Baltinglass and Tara and Knowth. The excavations at Knowth in the last few years have shown what happened subsequently to this megalithic cemetery. In a fairly early stage of the first millennium AD a house or houses were constructed in the middle of the central barrow, and to give protection to this occupation the barrow was transformed into a citadel by the digging of two concentric penannular ditches. These had gone out of use by the sixth/seventh century, but the occupation of the site continued. There is a complex of five souterrains and three of these are linked on to the eastern megalithic chamber forming a very involved complex of underground structures. One of the souterrains yielded tenth-century Anglo-Saxon coins. The Irish settlement of the Knowth megaliths extended from the early centuries AD down to the twelfth century: the site was then taken over by the Normans and this settlement lasted until AD 1300. The excavator of Knowth, Dr George

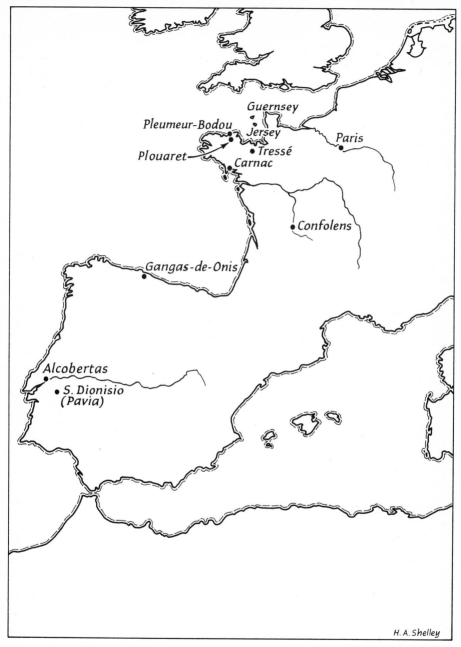

9 Sites of some of the megalithic monuments in France, Spain and Portugal mentioned in the text

Eogan, in supplying me with this information in advance of its full publication, comments, 'My guess is that the Passage Grave culture was so strong in Ireland that it left a lasting impression, and that by Iron Age times a number of the Passage Grave sites were sacred. Per, haps it was that the incoming Celts took over these already sacred sites in the belief that in so doing they would attain some special status. . . . After all it appears that those early Irish kings were probably more sacred than political figures.'

At the time of his much,regretted death in 1957 Professor Sean P. Ó Ríordáin was preparing to write the Rhys Lecture for the British Academy. I had given the lecture a few years before and called it 'Who were the Welsh?'. O Ríordáin said to me, 'If I write a lecture called "Who are the Irish?", I shall be forced to say that apart from a small veneer of Celtic,speaking chieftains and craftsmen, the Irish are basically the people of the Neolithic and Early Bronze Age who built the great megalithic tombs.' It had been O Ríordáin's curious fortune to excavate at Tara, and, at the Mound of the Hostages, to find a secondary burial of the second millennium B C, and, digging on in justifiable surprise, to discover that this mound, previously thought to be of the time of Patrick and the High Kings, had been originally built to cover a megalithic tomb, the radiocarbon date of its construc, tion, when calibrated, being about 2500 B C. Patrick visited the High King Loigaire at Tara and disputed there with the Druid Lucetmael three thousand years after some important prehistoric person had been buried in the Tara megalith. Here there must be some continuity with the elder faiths.

And what are we to make of the curious story of Patrick and the long grave? I quote from Dr James Carney's translation of Whitley Stokes's text of the *Vita Tripartita*: 'And Patrick came to Duchuil to a great grave, of astounding breadth and prodigious length which his *familia* had found. And with great amazement they marvelled that it extended 120 feet, and they said, "we do not believe this affair, that there was a man of this length." And Patrick answered and said, "If you wish you shall see him", and they said, "We do." And he struck

10 *Sites of some of the megalithic monuments in the British Isles mentioned in the text*

with his crozier a stone near its head, and signed the grave with the sign of the cross, and said "Open, O Lord, the grave." And the holy man opened the earth and the giant arose whole and said "Blessed be you, O holy man, for you have raised me even for one hour from many pains." Speaking so, he wept most bitterly, and said, "I will walk with you." They said, "We cannot allow you to walk with us, for men cannot look upon your face from fear of you. But believe in the God of Heaven and accept the baptism of the Lord, and you shall return to the place in which you were. And tell us of whom you are." [And the man said] "I am the son of the son of Cas, son of Glas, and was swineherd to King Lugar, king of Hirota. The warrior-band of the son of Mac Con slew me in the reign of Coirpe Nioth Fer, a hundred years ago today." And he was baptized and confessed God, and he fell silent, and was placed once more in his grave.'[6]

It was O. G. S. Crawford who first drew the attention of archaeologists to this remarkable passage, and he had no doubt what it meant: 'It is not generally known', he wrote, 'that the first recorded opening of a Long Barrow was carried out by St Patrick.'[7] Paul Ashbee supports this interpretation.[8] I do not accept the view that Patrick was dealing with a long barrow but he was surely dealing with some old, and possibly megalithic tomb. And this is not the only example. The *Life* goes on to recount how Patrick 'came to Findmag in the territory of the Ui Maini and he found there a marking Christian cross and two new graves. And from his car the holy man said "Who is it that is buried here?" And a voice from the grave said "I am a heathen man." The saint said "Why has a holy cross been set beside you?", and he replied "Because the mother of the man who is buried at my side asked that the sign of the cross be put by the grave of her son, but a stupid and foolish man put it by me." And Patrick springs out of his car and laid hold of the cross and pulled it from the heathen tomb and placed it over the head of the baptized man.'

I discussed these contacts of Patrick with the pagan past of Ireland with Dr Kathleen Hughes, Fellow of Newnham College and University Lecturer in Celtic. She points out that raisings from the dead are a

18

very common hagiographical theme but that she had been thinking for some while about the continuity between early episcopal and pagan sites. Her concern had been mainly with Iron Age sites 'wondering if the lands used to maintain pagan sanctuaries were made over to churches'. It seems likely that they were, and that some of them were older than the Iron Age in origin, going back to the elder megalithic faith.

Sir William Ridgeway tells a tale about a lonely spot in County Cork – Cnocan near Mallow, where there is a ring fort with a barrow outside. Until about 1870 there took place at this site an annual gather, ing for a fair, and foot,races were run alongside the mound. 'Then', writes Ridgeway, 'the landlord had the fair transferred to a village some four miles distant, but, though the fair was moved from a desolate spot to a thriving village, it has practically died out. [The thriving village, by the way, was Ballyclough.] Then came a road,contractor who thought that the barrow, which was made of pieces of the local lime, stone, would supply good cheap material for the roads.' He discovered a large stone cist or megalithic tomb in the barrow. Ridgeway con, cludes, 'It is clear why the foot,races had been held there year by year from the Bronze Age down to our own time. The old chief delighted in manhood when in life, so in death his spirit was honoured by the enactment of manly sports as the seasons revolved.'9

Ridgeway's tale is surely a good example of the survival into late historic times of pagan practices: it may support those of us who have suggested that the cursus monuments may have been used for what he calls 'manly sports' and one asks oneself if, by some strange dispensa, tion, one could see back into the past, would one see athletes or aco, lytes moving along the stone rows of Carnac? However that may be, there was, as Hadrian Allcroft once said, in Ireland 'no interlude of Constantinian Christianity between stark paganism and the mission of St Patrick'. I suspect, with Ó Ríordáin, that much of the stark paganism was pre,Iron Age. We should remember that the word 'pagan' itself comes from the Latin *paganus* meaning someone belong, ing to a *pagus*, namely a canton, county, district or village, and it was surely in the villages of the Roman Empire, as well as outside the bounds of that empire, in for example Ireland and Scandinavia, that the ancient beliefs of the villagers were most likely to survive either intact, or modi fied into new faiths.

The Celtic Church in Ireland clearly had to deal with the elder faiths. So had the Roman Church on the continent of Europe. The early Church Councils were much concerned with the worship of stones, and the edicts of Arles in 452, Tours in 567, Nantes in 658, and Toledo in 681 deal with these matters. The Arles Council of 452 decreed that 'if, in any diocese, any infidel either lighted torches, or worshipped trees, fountains or stones, or neglected to destroy them, he should be guilty of sacrilege'. At Tours in 567 the Council exhorted the clergy to excommunicate those who, at certain trees, stones or fountains, perpetrated things contrary to the ordinances of the Church. The oft-quoted decrees of Nantes in 658 – and Nantes, let us remember, is in good megalithic country – exhort 'Bishops and their servants to dig up and remove and hide to places where they cannot be found, those stones which in remote and woody places are still worshipped and where vows are still made.' The Twelfth Council at Toledo in 681 again inveighs against idolaters, so that the cult of fountains, stones and trees must have been continuing.

Of course the stones referred to in these injunctions are not necessarily megaliths, but some of them must be. And the evidence of the worrying survival of stone worship in early Christian Europe comes not only from Church Councils. St Martin, the first Bishop of Dumium, near Braga, the Apostle of the Sueves who worked for thirty years in Galicia, wrote, in 574, in his sermon *De correctione rusticorum* in which he showed that worship at stones survived into the sixth century, 'for what is lighting candles at stones but the worship of the devil'.[10] We should also remember here that in the closing years of the fourth century, St Pacianus, Bishop of Barcelona, wrote a book to combat the superstitious practice of people clothing themselves in the skins of deer and taking part in immoral rites, and the same abuse is con demned by St Caesarius of Arles whose dates are 470 to 540. It almost sounds as it Upper Palaeolithic rites were still being performed in early Christian western Europe.

It is not merely Church Councils and Bishops who were concerned with pagan worshippers in Christian times. An edict of Charlemagne from Aix-en-Chapelle dated 789 utterly condemns and execrates before God those trees, stones and fountains which foolish people worship. As late as the time of Canute there is a statute forbidding the barbarous adoration of the sun and moon, fire, fountains, trees and woods, stones and all kinds of devil-worship. Alfred denounced the *anfitheatra* of Britain as so many centres of devil-worship: he was referring presumably to Roman remains but might have included in his description sites like Avebury and Maumbury Rings. We should remember that Maumbury Rings in Dorchester, though owing something of its present shape to Cromwell and the Civil War, is a Roman amphitheatre built out of an earlier henge monument. At the end of St George Gray's excavations at Maumbury Rings, *The Times* published, in 1908, a remarkable dispatch on the site: it was written by

11 Maumbury Rings, Dorchester, Dorset

Thomas Hardy and, although its archaeology was sound enough, its most moving and dramatic passage was that which dealt with the execution there of Mrs Thomas Channing in March 1705/6. And one still wonders why Mrs Channing was hanged in a prehistoric temple.[11]

It was John Thurnam in his famous paper on long barrows who first drew attention to the curious passage in Felix's *Life of St Guthlac*.[12] Guthlac, who, according to the *Anglo-Saxon Chronicle* died in 714 at the age of forty-one, had been converted to Christianity after harrying the country at the head of a small war-band for nine years. He went to live as an anchorite in the Lincolnshire Fens. His biographer Felix, writing probably in the second quarter of the eighth century, seems to suggest that, as Dr J. N. L. Myres has argued, Guthlac was living in a plundered chambered barrow: but not, I think, as Thurnam argued, a megalithic tomb – it was probably a Roman barrow.[13] We remember here the well-known passage in *Beowulf* (lines 2200–2820) describing a dragon who lived in what was clearly a chambered barrow and guarded there much treasure. This account might possibly be based on an English prehistoric site, or could equally well be based on memories of Scandinavian and north German megalithic chambers. A. Keiller and S. Piggott argued that the passage refers to an Irish or Scottish chambered tomb because of the description of a stone arch, vault or bow, whereas all the megalithic tombs in Scandinavia and north Germany are roofed by capstones.[14]

It is well known that the Vikings did break into one great British megalithic monument, one with an arched, vaulted or bowed roof, namely Maes Howe in Orkney. There are twenty-four runic inscriptions at Maes Howe, as well as fine Viking representations of a dragon, a walrus and a serpent-knot. The inscriptions were made on several different occasions and include fourteen personal names. Their chief interest lies in the fact that they record that Norsemen on their way to the Crusades broke into Maes Howe and removed its treasure, whatever this may mean. This event is usually identified with the expedition of Earl Rognvald and Eindred the Younger, who wintered in Orkney 1150–51. There was another visit in January 1153 when Earl Harold

12 *Dragon incised by the Vikings on the walls of the Maes Howe megalithic monument in Orkney*

and his men landed near Stromness and were in the burial chamber 'when a snow storm drove over them, and there two men of their band lost their wits, and this was a great hindrance to their journey' – a laconic statement with which one may readily agree.[15]

I have a very special personal and private interest in St Samson, patron saint of Dol in the Ille-et-Vilaine department of Brittany. He was a pupil and disciple of St Illtyd in the Celtic monastery of Llanill-tud Fawr, now Llantwit Major, the village in the Vale of Glamorgan where my father was schoolmaster and where I was brought up. Samson's *Life* dates from the beginning of the seventh century and is one of the most authentic and reliable lives of a Celtic saint. Samson made a journey from Caldey to Ireland and then got to Cornwall, landing near the modern St Kew. He had with him in his boat a chariot or cart and in this he travelled across from St Kew to Fowey.

23

In this short transpeninsular journey he passed by a hill called 'Tri-curius', possibly Trig on the north-west flank of Bodmin Moor. There he and his party saw some people worshipping 'an abominable image'. Samson advanced and denounced them: he performed a miracle and they were baptized. 'On this hill', says his biographer, 'I myself have been . . . and with my hands have traced the sign of the cross which St Samson with his own hands carved by means of an iron instrument on a standing stone.'[16] This passage can only mean one thing: Samson saw people in the sixth century AD worshipping at a menhir. When he got from Fowey to Brittany he found himself in a country full of stand-ing stones: many of these today have crosses on them. The Christian-ized menhir at Trig in Cornwall does not survive.

13 *A Christianized menhir in Brittany*

14, 15 Two large Christianized menhirs in Brittany

Very gradually the Roman Church changed from forbidding the worship of stones, to absorbing the cult of megaliths into itself. Until the rule of Constantine the tendency had been to destroy heathen temples and their idols, but by the Edict of Theodosius pagan shrines were to be rededicated as Christian churches: and later the Edict of Honorius (AD 408) definitely forbade the demolition of heathen temples, at least in cities. As Sir Lawrence Gomme said many years ago in his *Folklore as an Historical Science*, 'Christianity was both antagonistic to, and tolerant of, pagan custom and belief. In principle and purpose it was antagonistic. In practice it was tolerant, where it could tolerate freely.'[17]

25

16 *The megalithic passage grave at Alcobertas, south Portugal, now part of a Christian church*

17 *Plan and section of the passage grave at Alcobertas, south Portugal*

18 *The megalithic tomb converted into a Christian church at San Dionisio, Portugal*

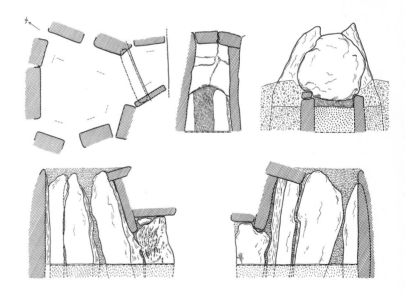

There are in central Portugal two very unusual megalithic monuments which show dramatically the free tolerance of the elder faiths:
one is the Anta de Alcobertas, Rio Maior, Extremadura, and the
other is the Anta-Capella of San Dionisio. Both are megalithic tombs
built four thousand years ago: both are now incorporated in Christian
churches of which they form side chapels.[18] In northern Spain, some
forty miles east of Oviedo, is the Church of Santa-Cruz de la Victoria
in the town of Gangas de Onis. Here the church is built on a mound
containing a passage grave, and the capstone of the megalithic tomb is
the altarstone of the church, a church built in the tenth/eleventh centuries. 'From this', writes Fergusson, 'it seems to be a fair inference that,
when the church was built on the mound, the dolmen was still a sacred
edifice of the aborigines. Had the Christians merely wanted a founda-
tion for their building, they would have filled up or destroyed the pagan
edifice.'[19]

19 *Large natural stones incorporated into the church of Arrichinaga, northern Spain*

Fergusson drew attention to another curious site in northern Spain, the Hermitage of S. Miguel at Arrichinaga, twenty-five miles from Bilbao. This site has been described as a megalithic monument, but it is not a man-made structure. It is a collection of large natural stones, but they have been Christianized, and I readily agree with Fergusson when he says 'the fact of these great stones being adopted by the Christians at all shows that they must have been considered sacred and objects of worship by the natives at the time when the Christians enclosed them in their edifice'.[20]

Mention has already been made of the curious monument on the island of Sainte-Marguerite at Confolens on the River Vienne. This

28

monument, now known as the 'Dolmen de la Chapelle', consists of a large capstone fourteen and a half feet long by twelve feet broad by three and a half feet thick, supported by four columns of Romanesque design with twelfth-century capitals. This site was originally a single simple rectangular chamber: each pillar was inserted separately under the capstone and the site was translated into a Christian chapel. On the underside of the capstone you will find today two incised symbols – a cross and a hafted axe. Here indeed, in art and architecture, the elder faith and Christianity appear to be wedded.

20 *The Dolmen de la Chapelle, Saint-Germain, Confolens, France*

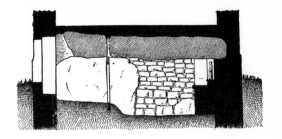

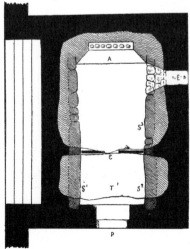

21 The Chapelle des Sept-Saints,
Plouaret, France. Sections and plan

22 The Chapelle des Sept-Saints,
Plouaret, France. Outside view

A. de Mortillet

The Dolmen de la Chapelle at Confolens is, admittedly, significant
and odd, but it is a fossil. The Chapelle des Sept-Saints in north
Brittany is no fossil and Mass is regularly celebrated in an *allée couverte*,
a long megalithic tomb. The hamlet of Les Sept-Saints is in the commune of Vieux-Marché, Lannion, Côtes-du-Nord. It is three miles
north-east of Plouaret and the present church was built between 1702
and 1714 – perhaps, say some, certainly, say others, on the site of an
older church. The church has a simple plan of a Latin cross with two
transepts: the south transept is an *allée couverte* sixteen feet long by seven
feet wide by five feet high, roofed by two large capstones. The monument is divided into two parts and in the altar niche are seven roughly
carved figures which represent the seven saints reportedly found in this
tomb.

While we are remembering the surprising fact of the Chapelle des
Sept-Saints at Plouaret, let us not forget the many examples of Christian

23 *The Tumulus de Saint-Michel, Carnac, Brittany*

churches built on megalithic barrows: for example the Tumulus de Saint-Michel at Carnac and the church on La Hougue Bie in Guernsey in the Channel Islands. Of course these may merely mean the utilization of good sites and have nothing to do with the survival of old sanctities. St Patrick may have used the Mound of the Hostages only because it was a nice mound with no historical or sacred significance. I do not think so and I do not think the churches on the Tumulus de Saint-Michel at Carnac and La Hougue Bie in Guernsey are accidents. In the small town of Carnac itself there is a free-standing dolmen with a Christian cross on it, and in many parts of Brittany there are Christianized menhirs. The most famous of the Breton Christianized menhirs is that of Pleumeur-Bodou, Perros-Guirec, Lannion in the Côtes-du-Nord, not so very far away from the Chapelle des Sept-Saints.

24 *The Dolmen de la Belle-Vue, Carnac, Morbihan, Brittany*

25 *The Christianized menhir at Pleumeur-*
Bodou, France

26 *The statue-menhir from Le Câtel,*
    Guernsey

27 *La Grandmère de la Chimquière in the*
    churchyard of St Martin's, Guernsey

Let us not forget here the two statue-menhirs that stand in church-
yards in the Channel Islands. One is at Le Câtel and the other is the
Grandmère de la Chimquière. These may not both date back to
megalithic times, and certainly the Grandmère has been remodelled
in Roman or medieval times, but La Câtel looks very much like the
sculptured slabs in the *allées couvertes* of the Paris Basin. My view is that
it is not a statue-menhir but a walling stone of a long tomb. This interpretation of the Le Câtel stone is not important: what is important is
that in two churches in 'Les Iles Anglo-Normandes', as the French
very properly call what we call the Channel Islands, there stand in
Christian ground pagan statues, and that they receive every year offer-
ings from the faithful. But what faithful? One asks what are these
twentieth-century people faithful to? As they put their pennies on the
head of the mother-goddess at Le Câtel and walk on to Mass in the
church, are they, unconsciously perhaps, making peace with two gods,
and placating the elder faiths?

34

Are there comparable examples in Britain of what happened in Iberia and France, namely the resolution of paganism into Christianity? Some scholars have said firmly no. Baldwin Brown was one of these: he wrote, 'there is no known instance in Britain where a Christian church has replaced a heathen fane'.[21] Professor Leo Borst of Buffalo who, admittedly, has very eccentric views about megaliths and no sure knowledge of them, nevertheless – and unfortunately encouraged by the Editor of *Nature* in one of his undiscriminating moments – strongly opposes Baldwin Brown. Borst thinks he finds traces of henge monuments under every cathedral he visits.

Neither Baldwin Brown nor Borst is right. A few religious buildings in Britain *are* associated with megaliths. Avebury is often quoted in this context but we should remember that, while part of the village is inside the prehistoric henge monument, the church is next door to it.

28 The henge monument at Avebury, Wiltshire

At Knowlton in Dorset we have a different story: here the church is inside a prehistoric henge monument. I wrote to Mr Collin Bowen of the Royal Commission on Historical Monuments (England) for his views on Knowlton, which we had visited together in 1971, and he replied, 'There is no surface or documentary indication of a pre-12th-century Church at Knowlton and there are no "megaliths" embodied in the fabric. I think there is little doubt that the Church was put in the henge deliberately to Christianize it. The deliberateness of the placing is emphasized by the knowledge we now have that Knowlton village was situate, as most usual, by a stream, whereas the Church and henge are on the highest local crest 600 yds away. The site must have been even more impressive when 26 barrows, destroyed in Victorian times, were still standing a quarter of a mile to the north on the opposite side of a shallow combe.'

29 *Two henge monuments at Knowlton, Dorset: one is ploughed out, the other has a Christian church inside*

The three stones of a stone circle incorporated in the circular wall of the Church of Yspytty Cynfyn, near Aberystwyth, Wales

In Wales, not far from Aberystwyth in Cardiganshire is the well-known site of Yspytty Cynfyn: here is a circular churchyard with three megaliths in the circular bank round the churchyard. It has often been claimed as an authentic example of a Christian church in a stone circle but from time to time doubts have been cast on its authenticity. Present-day opinion inclines to the view that it is the remains of a genuine stone circle.[22] Twenty miles away lies the Church of Llanfairpwll-gwyngyll, and here, as Professor Emrys Bowen has recently reminded us, there was a menhir underneath the pulpit of the church.[23]

What do Knowlton and Yspytty Cynfyn and Llanfairpwllgwyn-gyll mean? Do they mean a survival of sanctity of megalithic sites until the Middle Ages? I have no doubt myself that a knowledge of some facts about megaliths and the faith of the megalith-builders survived through the Roman period and the Migration period into the Christian Middle Ages. How else can we explain those strange sentences in Geoffrey of Monmouth's *History of the Kings of Britain*, written in the twelfth century? I refer to the statements that Merlin brought the stones

of Stonehenge from Ireland, and that the people who built such monuments in Ireland came from Africa. Whether Geoffrey had a *vetus-
tissimus liber* or not is unimportant: I cannot believe that he invented the
idea that the stones of Stonehenge came from the west or that the megalith-builders of Ireland came from the Mediterranean. The transfer
of the blue or foreign stones of Stonehenge from the Preseli Hills of
Pembrokeshire, argued, I think successfully, by H. H. Thomas to be
done by man, and unsuccessfully, recently, by Kellaway to be by ice-
action, was a great event in the prehistory of southern Britain. It was
surely the transfer of a sacred site from west Wales to Salisbury Plain
that Geoffrey of Monmouth was writing about.[24]

Geoffrey was probably using surviving folk-memory. The antiquaries of the Renaissance looked at our ancient monuments afresh
with no guides except Classical writers and the Bible: it is not surprising that they 'restored' our megalithic monuments to giants, fairies,
Samson, King Arthur, the Danes, the Romans, the Phoenicians, but
most of all to the Druids of the Ancient Britons. Out of this romantic
Druidic preoccupation with megaliths there developed a general
interest in these ancient stone structures, not only among antiquaries
like John Aubrey, Edward Lhuyd, William Stukeley and Henry
Rowlands but among the builders of follies and grottoes. Professor
Stuart Piggott has suggested that John Wood's plan of the Circus
and associated streets in Bath was based on Inigo Jones's plan of
Stonehenge in his book of 1655.[25]

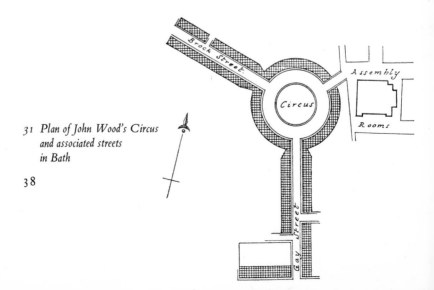

31 *Plan of John Wood's Circus
and associated streets
in Bath*

38

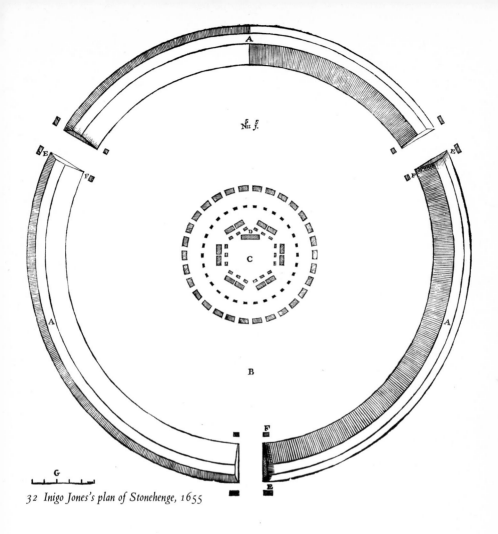

32 *Inigo Jones's plan of Stonehenge, 1655*

In an alcove in the wall on the west side of the Fosse Way, two miles north of Batheaston, where Somerset, Gloucestershire and Wiltshire meet, is a curious structure called the 'Three Shire Stones'. Here are three uprights supporting a capstone: inside is a broken boundary-stone bearing the date 1736, and on the two-inch manuscript map of the district at the Ordnance Survey (dated 1813–14) there is a note

33 *The 'Three Shire Stones', a modern megalith built 1736 but probably using prehistoric stones. It now marks the place where Gloucestershire, Somerset and Wiltshire meet*

saying 'Shires Stones erected 1736.' Crawford believed this structure to be 'a modern imitation of a dolmen'.[26] The so-called 'Tetralithon' on the Petersfield-Winchester road is a strange affair: on one side of the road there is a large heap of stones in a beech copse, the tomb of a racehorse with silver shoes – across the road there is a little four-foot henge: three groups of boulders overgrown with brambles.

In 1792 Lord Arundel employed Josiah Lane to make a grotto for him at Wardour Castle in Wiltshire. Lane was a celebrated constructor of rock-work and his grotto at Wardour is a charming and remarkable structure. Here is Barbara Jones's account of it from her fascinating book *Follies and Grottoes*: 'Built on a brick basis, it is of tufa and stone with the occasional ammonite, now covered with green moss and long ferns, for it is in a very sheltered and gloomy situation. The plan is most cunning, turning in and out with many views through jagged holes into other parts. The dark yews and the bank which it is built against,

40

and the pattern book construction, make it the most Gothic of Grot-toes.'[27] What is particularly interesting is that Josiah Lane had used in his rock-work part of a megalithic tomb – that from Place Farm, Tisbury; three monoliths of this tomb were removed in 1792 for use in Wardour Castle. Geoffrey Grigson wrote in a letter to me, 'One mono-lith is still there so the rock-work is a meeting place of Druids, Chinese gardeners and the Cumaean Sybil.'

In the very next parish to Wardour, at Fonthill, Beckford had 'an imitation cromlec' set up in his grounds, but this, like his house and tower, and most of the curiosities in the grounds, are almost entirely destroyed. In 1814 the fifteenth Earl of Shrewsbury began the construc-tion of a house and landscape at Alton in Staffordshire: after his death in 1827 the work was carried on by his nephew. Among other oddities it contains what is often described as an imitation Stonehenge, but, more accurately and descriptively, 'The Druid's Sideboard'. It is a very strange construction of piled stones and megalithic slabs.[28]

34 'The Druid's Sideboard', a mock megalithic construction in the grounds of the Earl of Shrewsbury's estate at Alton, Staffordshire

35 'Merlin's Grotto', Cobham Park, Kent

There is an early Victorian Stonehenge adjoining the park at The Quinta, Weston Rhyn in Shropshire. In the early nineteenth century the Earl of Darnley had removed the stones of an entire megalithic monument and re-erected them to form what was described as 'a Merlin's Grotto' in Cobham Park, Kent.

But the strangest and finest mock-megalith in Britain is surely the temple on the Yorkshire Moors at Ilton, near Masham. This was built in the 1820s to the order of William Danby of Swinton Hall. Finding the local people out of work and wishing to help them, he preferred to provide them with jobs rather than give them dole out of charity. He got them to build what he called a Druids' temple and paid them each a shilling a day. The result is very remarkable, with a grotto at the far end cut into the hillside, and several dolmens and trilithons built outside the main enclosure in the surrounding countryside.[29] The great

42

36 One of the mock dolmens forming
part of the Druids' Temple,
Masham, Yorkshire

37 Druids' Temple, Masham, Yorkshire,
built 1820

38 Impression of the Druids' Temple, Masham, Yorkshire

39 The megalithic site of the 'Mont de la Ville', St Helier, Jersey

follies of George Henry Law, Bishop of Bath and Wells from 1824 to 1854, at Banwell in Somerset, are well known. The woods were replanted by the Bishop: every fifty yards there are pairs of standing stones, one on each side, leading up to the Belvedere Tower which he built in 1835. In the bone cave there is a semicircular room with five niches cut in the rock, coffin-shaped but comfortable. Between two arches the eccentric Bishop had inscribed this verse

> *Here where once druids trod in times of yore*
> *And stain'd their altars with a victim's gore*
> *Here now the Christian ransomed from above*
> *Adores a God of mercy and of love.*

Professor Ole Klindt-Jensen has noted the same tendencies in Scandi-navia in the eighteenth century, a Romantic style of landscape-design with prehistoric motifs and hermits' cells, and fake prehistoric monu-ments such as the barrow surrounded by a massive stone ring in the park at Moesgaard near Aarhus, or 'the enigmatic relic from Antiquity' (actually a dolmen complete with antique busts) designed by Wiede-welt for the palace garden at Fredensborg.[30]

We must mention here the megalithic monument at Park Place near Henley. It is not a mock-megalith or folly; it is a genuine antiquity but has no right to be in southern Britain. In August 1785 a Colonel of the St Helier Militia in Jersey was having a piece of land levelled for a parade-ground somewhere on the site later occupied by the Fort Regent.

45

The men digging came across a megalithic monument usually called the 'Mont de la Ville'. It was offered to the Governor of Jersey, Marshall Conway, by the Vingtaine de la Ville as a gift from the island he had served so well. He hesitated to accept this unusual present especially when he learnt he would have to pay for the cost of transporting the megalith. Horace Walpole wrote to him, 'Pray do not disappoint me but transport the Cathedral of your island to your domain on our continent.' In March 1788 the stones, stowed in a barge, passed up the Thames to Conway's house outside Henley. Horace Walpole took a great interest in the proceedings and said that the monument had been correctly assembled, but this is doubtful. The monument now stands on a hill overlooking the Thames: it bears a simple inscription: 'Cet ancien Temple des Druides découvert le 12me Aout 1785 sur le Montagne de St Helier dans l'Isle de Jersey, a été presenté par les Habitans à son Excellence le General Conway, leur Gouverneur'.[31]

40 The megalithic monument, 'Mont de la Ville', as re-erected in Park Place, Henley

Other genuine megaliths have made curious journeys in historical times, and I am not here referring to the transport of monuments for their own good into the courtyards of museums in Copenhagen, Tiflis, Saint-Germain-en-Laye, Penmarc'h, La Rochelle, Troyes, and Algiers, to mention only a few. I am thinking of the megalithic tombs in the cemeteries of Confolens and Meudon. The modern cemetery at Confolens is only a few miles away from the Dolmen de la Chapelle on the island of Sainte-Marguerite to which we have already referred: in the modern cemetery there now stands the Dolmen de Périssac formerly at Essé. It was bought for a hundred francs in 1892 and re-erected in the cemetery to act as a tomb for a lady much addicted to dolmens. Her body was placed in a carved sarcophagus set on top of the capstone.

In the Cimetière des Essarts at Meudon outside Paris one comes with surprise on a reconstructed rectangular megalithic tomb that used to be the Dolmen de Kerhan in the commune of Saint-Philibert in the Morbihan. It was excavated in 1886 by Gaillard and moved to Paris ten years later to form the tomb of the family Piketti. A plaque commemorates the fact that since it was moved from Brittany it has still been used as a collective tomb, and that nine members of the Piketti family have been buried in the ground beneath the tomb.[32]

The activities of the folly-builders and grotto-merchants, and those who purchased old megaliths to make new tombs, stand apart from the work of those involved in the Welsh Gorsedd of Bards. The Eisteddfod is an ancient institution in Welsh life; its revival dates from the end of the eighteenth century. It had in its historical contexts nothing to do with megaliths and Druids. This was grafted on largely due to Edward Williams, Iolo Morgannwg as he called himself. He was a self-educated journeyman mason of Cowbridge in the Vale of Glamorgan: his dates were 1747 to 1826. He was a remarkable man and a very learned one but he had a perverse tendency to invent for Welsh literature an imaginary past. The strangest of his fabrications is the Gorsedd of the Bards. About 1780 he began to create the pattern of an ancient romantic Glamorgan which was entirely in his own imagination. He then began to link his

42 The Dolmen de Kerhan in the process of being transported from Brittany to Paris to form the Piketti family tomb at Meudon

43, 44 The Piketti tomb in the Cimitière des Essarts, Meudon, Paris. It was originally the Dolmen de Kerhan in Morbihan (see ill. 42)

45 *Gorsedd circle in front of the National Museum of Wales, Cardiff*

invented customs with the known existence of Druids. He asserted that the succession of Druidical lore had been maintained unbroken in Glamorgan from prehistoric times to the eighteenth century AD: he claimed that there were by then only two people who were ordained Bards of the old tradition. These were a Mr Edward Evans of Aberdare, and, not surprisingly, himself. He revealed all these fancies to the London Welsh, and organized for them the first Gorsedd of the Bards on Primrose Hill on 21 June 1792.

He threw down a circle of pebbles at his ceremony on Primrose Hill, and these served as a miniature stone circle for his rites. In 1819 he attended the Eisteddfod in Carmarthen and took with him the pebbles he had used on Primrose Hill twenty-seven years before. He set them out as a circle on the grass lawn of the Ivy Bush Hotel, surrounded by attend-ant Bards who wore ribbons on their arms. It was, by all accounts, quite an occasion. By the middle of the nineteenth century the Gorsedd of Bards got firmly attached to the Eisteddfod. Traditions are readily made and it was soon an article of faith to many Welshmen that the Gorsedd of Bards had been part of the Eisteddfod for all time and was in some way a survival of the Druids. Sir John Morris Jones pointed out the true history of all this in 1896, but still every year a stone circle is built

CYNLLUN CYLCH YR ORSEDD.

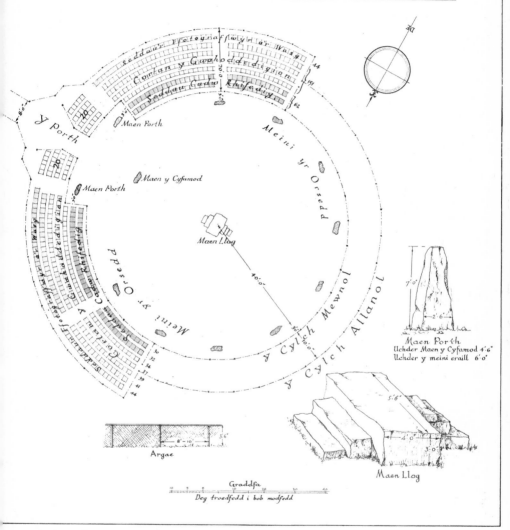

46 Plan used in construction of Gorsedd circles for the Welsh Eisteddfod

47 Queen Elizabeth II, when Princess Elizabeth, being initiated into the Gorsedd of Bards

somewhere in Wales and the Gorsedd parades around, the Ovates in green robes, the Bards in blue, and the Druids in white carrying regalia designed by Sir Hubert Herkomer.[33]

The Gorsedd of Bards of Wales happens only at these modern mega- lithic circles constructed in the last hundred years. The Cornish Bards on the other hand actually use prehistoric monuments. On 4 September 1948, for example, the Twenty-first Cornish Gorsedd took place at the megalithic tomb of Caerwynen near Camborne. And it appears that it is not only Bards and neo-Druids who use old and new megaliths. Grinsell has drawn attention to the fact that in the Museum of Witch- craft at Boscastle in Cornwall, there is a witch's split-ended hazel wand, used at the Rollright Stones at dawn on 1 May 1955; this illustrates, as

48 *Gathering of Welsh Bards at the Gorsedd*

he says, the latter-day revival of witch covens, and the occasional choice
of prehistoric sites for their meetings.[34]

It is worth recollecting here that through the centuries in various
places people have been building structures with large flat stones which
on the grounds of size justify the name megaliths, but which have
nothing to do with the original prehistoric megaliths or with the mock-
megaliths of the eighteenth and nineteenth centuries. The clapper bridges
of Dartmoor are megalithic structures, though not prehistoric as the Post
Office mistakenly thought a few years ago when they displayed one on a
stamp. In western Wales there are many pigsties built of megaliths. Then
there is a megalithic seat in Dunnabridge Pound on Dartmoor which
was originally said to be the President's Chair of the Stannaries Court

53

49 *The Dolmen de la Pierre-Folle at Bournan, Touraine, France, now used as cowshed and barn*

50 *The great* allée *couverte of Bagneux at Saumur, France, which served for years as a barn, garage and café*

51 *Megalithic tomb of La Madeleine, near Les Rosiers, Touraine, France, converted into a cowshed*

52 *Small statue of the Virgin, in a plastic container, set in a dolmen*

on Crockern Tor.[35] We should also remember that in recent times many French megalithic tombs have been used as barns, storage places for farm implements, bakehouses and even garages; and that occasionally one still comes across some modern Christian offering in a megalith, like the Virgin in a plastic container which my wife and I discovered in a megalithic tomb in the Ardèche. And ordinary megalithic construc‑ tion during historical times is the answer to Mystery Hill at North Salem in New Hampshire. It is some forty miles north of Boston, and as you approach it, a large notice says 'Welcome to Mystery Hill – the American Stonehenge'. It is an extensive site of old farm buildings and perhaps a folly or two. Carbon 14 dating shows that the site did have an early occupation of about 2000 BC – a settlement of native American Indians. Even so, I share Dr Hugh Hencken's views that the visible structures of the present day are unlikely to be earlier than the seventeenth century AD and have no real formal or constructional resemblances to the great megalithic monuments of prehistoric western Europe.[36]

53 'Mystery Hill', North Salem, New Hampshire. Though the site is prehistoric the visible buildings are probably no earlier than the seventeenth century AD

54 'Stonehenge' erected at Maryhill, Washington, as a war memorial

55 Panel in the wall of the new Chemistry Laboratory in Cambridge, depicting megaliths and alchemical symbols

But there *is* an American Stonehenge; it was built by Samuel Hill as a First World War memorial at Maryhill, Washington, and the tradi⁄tion of building mock⁄megaliths continues. When, in 1958, the scaf⁄folding was removed from the new Chemistry Laboratory in Cam⁄bridge, there was revealed a panel of megaliths decorated with the arms of the University of Cambridge, and five alchemical symbols. Mr John Murray Easton, the architect, wrote to me: 'I am glad you are interested . . . whether or not you approve of this "megalithic oddity". It arose from the usual mixture of reasons. Some sort of panel in this position was indicated, for no windows were wanted there. . . . I have always been intrigued by the mysterious urge that compelled people to do what they did in megalithic times from Mycenae to the stone men of Male⁄kula. . . . Then I have a liking for stones quâ stones.'

SUR LE FRONT
STEENSTRATE, LANGEMARK,
ST. JULIEN LA 87°D.I.T. ET LA
45° D.I.FRANÇAISE ONT SUBI LE
22 AVRIL 1915 A 17 HEURES LA
PREMIÈRE ATTAQUE ALLEMANDE
PAR LES GAZ ASPHYXIANTS.

HERINNERING AAN DE 87°FR.T.I.D.
EN DE 45°FR.I.D.DIE HIER OP
22 APRIL 1915 TE 17 U.DE EERSTE
GASAANVAL DOORSTONDEN

IEPERS KWARTIER   GEMEENTE BOEZINGE

56 *The 'Calvaire-Dolmen' near Poperinghe, Belgium, erected to commemorate the first use of gas by the Germans in 1915*

57 *The commemorative plaque on the 'Calvaire-Dolmen' in Belgium*

My wife and I visited one of the strangest modern megaliths only a few months ago. We were intrigued by an entry on the Michelin map of south Belgium; it marked a 'Calvaire-Dolmen' a few miles from Poperinghe. When we got there we found at the side of the road a calvary and a dolmen, put up to commemorate the first use of gas by the Germans in 1915 against the French and Belgians.

Where have we got to in this brief inquiry? I suggest three things emerge. First, that in the last three centuries there has been a minor taste for megaliths, which began when they could be affectionately seen through romantic and Druidical spectacles. Second, that the use of large stones for walling, roofing and bridging happened in the Middle Ages and had nothing to do with prehistoric megaliths. But third, and this is

58

important, there surely was a survival of some feeling of sacredness about megaliths into post-Roman and Christian times. The building of a church in a henge monument at Knowlton, the incorporation of megaliths into Christian churches at San Dionisio, Alcobertas, Gangas de Onis, Confolens and Plouaret, and the Christianization of menhirs – all this is not conscious antiquarianism. If the original mega-lithic monuments were built between 4000 and 2000 BC it is hardly surprising that beliefs which lasted for two thousand years and more should not have died out entirely. But they would have to survive through the two immediately pre-Roman millennia when other faiths were practised. But were these other faiths completely different? In an extreme-ly important passage written fifteen years ago, Professor Christopher Hawkes saw the evolution of prehistoric religious beliefs in France and Britain as an accommodation of the 'masculine sky-religion' of the Indo-Europeans with 'the old chthonic megalithic one existing here before them, which could descend through the Bronze Age to their undisputedly Celtic successors. Thence came the religion that the Druids administered.'[37] The Druids of protohistory may quite well be the priesthood of the earlier megalithic religion. It would be an amusing turn round of our thinking if, having scoffed in a superior way at Aubrey, Stukeley and Rowlands for restoring the megaliths to the Druids, we are now restoring the Druids of history to the megaliths of prehistory. This may be too blunt a way of putting it, but I find it difficult to envisage why there should be a Christian occupation of some megalithic sites, unless a real tradition of their importance as special and sacred places was carried through the period of the Bronze Age and Early Iron of barbarian Europe and into historic times.

NOTES

1 On the present dating of megalithic monuments see P. R. Giot, *Proceedings of the Prehistoric Society*, XXXVII, part II, 1971, 208–17; Henrik Tauber, *Antiquity*, XLVI, 1972, 106–10; and Colin Renfrew, *Antiquity*, XLVI, 1972, 141–4.

2 *Revue mensuelle de l'École d'Anthropologie de Paris*, XI, 1897, 321–38.

3 See S. P. Ó Ríordáin and G. E. Daniel, *New Grange and the Bend of the Boyne* (London 1964), Chapter V.

4 I owe this reference to the late Mrs N. K. Chadwick, *Early Brittany* (Cardiff 1969).

5 R. J. C. Atkinson, *Stonehenge* (Harmondsworth 1960).

6 J. Carney, *The Problem of St Patrick* (Dublin 1961).

7 *Antiquity*, X, 1936, 479.

8 *The Earthen Long Barrow in Britain* (London 1969).

9 Ridgeway records this story in his *The Origin of Tragedy* (Cambridge 1910), 35, and his *The Early Age of Greece* (Cambridge 1901), 545. See also A. Hadrian Allcroft, *The Circle and the Cross*, II (London 1930), 20–1.

10 Stephen K. McKenna, *Paganism and Pagan Survivals in Spain up to the Fall of the Visigothic Kingdom* (Washington 1938).

11 Thomas Hardy's account of Maumbury Rings was published in *The Times*, 9 October 1908, 11, and reprinted in H. Orel (ed.), *Thomas Hardy's Personal Writings* (London 1967) 225–32.

12 J. Thurnam, *Archaeologia*, 1868, 204.

13 G. E. Daniel, *The Prehistoric Chamber Tombs of England and Wales* (Cambridge 1950), 22–3.

14 A. Keiller and S. Piggott, *Antiquity*, XIII, 1939, 360–61.

15 Royal Commission on the Ancient and Historical Monuments of Scotland, *Inventory of Orkney and Shetland, II (Orkney)* (Edinburgh 1946), 309–13.

16 For St Samson see E. G. Bowen, in *Aberystwyth Studies*, XIII, 1934, 61–7; S. Baring-Gould and J. Fisher, *Lives of the British Saints*, IV, 1913, 130–70; and T. Taylor, *The Life of St Samson of Dol* (London 1925).

17 *Folklore as an Historical Science* (London 1908), 321.

18 Georg and Vera Leisner, *Die Megalithgräber der Iberischen Halbinsel* (Berlin 1943 and 1956).

19 James Fergusson, *Rude Stone Monuments in all Countries: their Age and Uses* (London 1872), 387.

20 Fergusson, *ibid.*, 388.

21 G. Baldwin Brown, *The Arts in Early England*, I (London 1903), 269.

22 When W. F. Grimes wrote his *South Wales*, No. 5 in the *Megalithic Survey* of the Ordnance Survey (1936), he expressed his doubts as to the authenticity of Yspytty Cynfyn as the remains of a genuine stone circle, as had been claimed by many, for example, Fleure and Peake in *The Way of the Sea* (Oxford 1929), 91.

23 *Antiquity*, XLV, 1971, 213.

24 On Geoffrey of Monmouth and his sources see S. Piggott, *Antiquity*, XV, 1941, 269–86 and 305–19.

25 On Wood, the plan of Bath and Stonehenge see S. Piggott, *The Druids*, London, 1968, 149–53.

26 O. G. S. Crawford, *The Long Barrows of the Cotswolds*, Gloucester, 1925, 227–8.

27 Barbara Jones, *Follies and Grottoes* (London 1953), 243.

28 *Ibid.*, 120.

29 *Ibid.*, 127–9.

30 O. Klindt-Jensen, *The History of Scandinavian Archaeology* (London, in the press).

31 J. Hawkes, *The Archaeology of the Channel Islands: II, The Bailiwick of Jersey* (London 1939), 240–42; Barbara Jones, *op. cit.*, 121–2.

32 G. E. Daniel, *The Prehistoric Chamber Tombs of France* (London 1960), 220.

33 S. Piggott, *The Druids*, 164–9; G. E. Daniel, *Antiquity*, XXXV, 1961, 260–62; Thomas Parry, *The Story of the Eisteddfod*, Liverpool (n.d.).

34 *Antiquity*, XLVI, 1972, 59.

35 A. Hadrian Allcroft, *The Circle and the Cross*, I (London 1927), 360 and Fig. 35.

36 H. O'N. Hencken, *New England Quarterly*, XII, 1939; G. E. Daniel, *Antiquity*, XLVI, 1972, 2.

37 C. F. C. Hawkes in (ed. J. M. Wallace-Hadrill and J. McManners), *France: Government and Society* (London 1957), 16; see also Christopher and Jacquetta Hawkes, *Prehistoric Britain*, Harmondsworth, 1937, 161–162.

LIST AND SOURCES OF ILLUSTRATIONS

1 Drawing of Stonehenge by Eckhardt in 1750.
2 Oblique air view of the alignments at Carnac, Morbihan, France. *Photo Lapie – Photothèque Française.*
3 Menhirs near Carnac, Morbihan, France. *Photo by Roger Viollet of old drawing by Queyroy.*
4 Air view of temple complex at Haġar Qim, Malta. *Photo courtesy Professor J.D. Evans.*
5 *Allée couverte* at Essé near Rennes, Brittany, France. *Photo Ruth Daniel*
6 Dolmen in Charente, France. *Photo Ruth Daniel.*
7 Air view of cemetery at Lough Crew, County West Meath, Ireland. *Photo Dr J.K. St Joseph, University of Cambridge.*
8 Corbelled roof in passage grave at New Grange, Ireland. *Photo S.P. Ó Ríordáin.*
9 Map showing some megalithic sites in France, Spain and Portugal. *Drawing by H.A. Shelley.*
10 Map showing some megalithic sites in the British Isles. *Drawing by H.A. Shelley.*
11 Air view of Maumbury Rings, Dorchester, Dorset. *Photo courtesy Dr J.K. St Joseph, Crown copyright reserved.*
12 Dragon incised on walls of megalithic monument at Maes Howe, Orkney. Drawing after Fergusson, *Rude Stone Monuments*, London 1872.
13 Christianized menhir, Brittany, France.
14 Christianized menhir, Brittany, France. *Photo Roger Viollet.*
15 Christianized menhir, Brittany, France.
16 Megalithic passage grave at Alcobertas forming part of Christian church. *Photo G. and V. Leisner.*
17 Plan and sections of the Alcobertas passage grave. After G. and V. Leisner.
18 Megalithic tomb at San Dionisio, Portugal, converted into a Christian church. *Photo G. and V. Leisner.*
19 Natural stones forming part of structure of church at Arrichinaga, Spain. After Fergusson, *Rude Stone Monuments*, London 1872.
20 Dolmen de la Chapelle, SaintGermain, Confolens, Charente, France. *Photo Archives Photographiques, Paris.*
21, 22 Church of Les SeptSaints, Plouaret, CôtesduNord, France, sections and plan, and outside view. After A. de Mortillet.
23 Tumulus de SaintMichel, Carnac, Brittany, France. *Photo Lapie – Photothèque Française.*
24 Dolmen de la BelleVue, Route de Menec, Carnac, Morbihan, Brittany, France. *Photo Editions Gaby.*
25 Christianized menhir at PleumeurBodou, CôtesduNord, France.
26 Statuemenhir from Le Câtel, Guernsey, Channel Islands.
27 La Grandmère de la Chimquière: modified statuemenhir in the churchyard of St Martin's, Guernsey, Channel Islands.

28 Air view of henge monument at Avebury, Wiltshire. *Photo courtesy Department of the Environment, Crown copyright reserved.*

29 Air view of two henge monuments at Knowlton, Dorset. *Photo Dr J.K. St Joseph, University of Cambridge.*

30 Three stones of a stone circle incorporated in the circular wall of the Church of Yspytty Cynfyn, near Aberystwyth, Cardiganshire, Wales.

31 Plan of the Circus and associated streets in Bath, Somerset, designed by John Wood. *Drawing by Mrs D.D.A. Simpson, reproduced by kind permission of Sir John Summerson and the Cresset Press.*

32 Plan of Stonehenge by Inigo Jones, 1655. *Drawing by Mrs D.D.A. Simpson.*

33 The 'Three Shire Stones', marking the boundary between Gloucestershire, Somerset and Wiltshire. Built in the eighteenth century with what may be prehistoric stones.

34 'The Druid's Sideboard', Alton, Staffordshire. Drawing by Barbara Jones in *Follies and Grottoes*, London 1953.

35 Megalithic monument re-erected in the early nineteenth century in Cobham Park, Kent. *Photo Ruth Daniel.*

36 One of the mock dolmens at the Druids' Temple, Masham, Yorkshire. *Photo Ruth Daniel.*

37 Druids' temple at Masham; North Riding of Yorkshire, built 1820. *Photo Ruth Daniel.*

38 Drawing of the Druids' Temple at Masham, by Barbara Jones in *Follies and Grottoes*, London 1953.

39 Megalithic site of the 'Mont de la Ville', St Helier, Jersey, Channel Islands from a coloured etching by George Heriot, *c.* 1785.

40 The Mont de la Ville, the megalithic monument formerly in Jersey, set up in Park Place, Henley.

41 Modern tomb in the cemetery of Confolens, Charente, France, re-using a prehistoric dolmen. Photo R. Burnard, published in *The Reliquary and Illustrated Archaeologist.*

42 The Dolmen de Kerhan, Morbihan, France on its way from Brittany to Paris, for use as the Piketti family tomb at Meudon. *Photo Archives Photographiques de France.*

43, 44 Two views of the Piketti tomb in the Cimetière des Essarts, Meudon, Paris, to form which the Dolmen de Kerhan was brought from Morbihan. *Photos Ruth Daniel.*

45 Modern Gorsedd circle in front of the National Museum of Wales, Cathays Park, Cardiff. *Photo courtesy National Museum of Wales.*

46 Plan used in the construction of the modern Gorsedd circles for the Welsh Eisteddfod. *Courtesy the Eisteddfod Office.*

47 Queen Elizabeth II, when Princess Elizabeth, being initiated into a Gorsedd of Bards at a modern megalithic circle.

48 Gorsedd of Welsh Bards in action.

49 The Dolmen de la Pierre-Folle at Bournan in the Touraine region of France, converted into a cowshed and barn.

50 *Allée couverte* of Bagneux in the suburbs of Saumur, on the Loire, used for years as a barn, garage and café. *Photo Roger Viollet.*

51 Megalithic tomb of La Madeleine,

63

near Rosiers in the Touraine region of France, now used as a cowshed. *Photo Ruth Daniel.*

52 Modern figurine representing the Virgin Mary, in a plastic container, set in a dolmen in the Ardèche region of France. *Photo Ruth Daniel.*

53 'Mystery Hill', North Salem, New Hampshire, U.S.A.

54 The 'Stonehenge' at Maryhill, Washington, U.S.A., erected as a memorial to American servicemen who fell in the First World War.

55 Panel depicting megaliths and alchemical symbols inserted in a wall of the Chemistry Laboratory, Lensfield Road, Cambridge, built in 1958. *Photo Edward Leigh.*

56 The 'Calvaire-Dolmen' beside the road from Roeselare to Poperinghe, Belgium. *Photo Ruth Daniel.*

57 Plaque on the 'Calvaire-Dolmen', commemorating the first use of gas by the Germans against the French and Belgians in 1915. *Photo Ruth Daniel.*

Illustrations 15, 25–27, 30, 33, 40, 47 and 48 are reproduced from slides provided by the Author.